RANGER RICK'S BEST FRIENDS

HI, I'M RANGER RICK, the official conservation symbol for young members of the National Wildlife Federation, and leader of the Ranger Rick Nature Clubs. On behalf of all the animals in Deep Green Wood, welcome to our world of nature and wildlife.

Lions and Tigers

by Jocelyn Arundel

LIONS AND TIGERS ARE AMAZING _____4

STORIES:

    1 Winda's Pride _____6

    2 Lucky Boto _____14

    3 The Eyes and Ears of a Tiger _____20

SAVING LIONS AND TIGERS _____28

WHERE LIONS AND TIGERS LIVE _____30

WHEN YOU SEE A LION OR A TIGER _____32

**Created and Published by
The National Wildlife Federation
Washington, D.C.**

Copyright © 1974 National Wildlife Federation
Standard Book Number 0-912186-12-7
Library of Congress Catalog Number 74-80049

LIONS AND TIGERS

THE LION IS BIGGER THAN ALL OTHER CATS, EXCEPT THE TIGER. Some say the tiger drove the lion out of Asia.

LIONS AND TIGERS ROAR. So do their closest cousins, leopards and jaguars. They can't purr the way all other cats, big and little, can. But purring cats can't roar!

ARE AMAZING

The **TEETH** of lions and tigers are good for tearing flesh, and their **JAWS** grip hard as a vise.

The **EYES** of lions and tigers—and leopards and jaguars—have **ROUND PUPILS**. All other cats have eyes with vertical slits.

Most cats, big and little, can turn **SHARP CLAWS INTO SOFT FEET** by pulling a toe joint upward to bury the pointed nails.

Of all the big cats, **ONLY LIONS LIVE AND MOVE IN** large groups, called **PRIDES**.

Winda's Pride

The lioness, Winda, came down from the limb where she had been resting. She slipped through grasses as high as her shoulder. With her keen amber eyes she could see antelopes grazing on the African plains. But today, Winda paid no attention to antelopes.

Holding him by the scruff of his neck, mother carries her wanderer home.

In Swahili, Winda's name means "to hunt," but just now Winda was not interested in hunting. She had her mind on a hidden place, a rocky cave protected by thorny bushes. She had chosen that spot to give birth.

Boto and three other cubs were born that night as the new moon rose. No bigger than collie puppies, they nestled close to Winda's belly, searching for milk.

Winda's tongue licked down each soft, spotted coat. A lion's tongue is rough, like a file. It can strip flesh from bone. Or it can soothe and cleanse. When Winda used her tongue, now, to tidy her little ones,

Soon to bear young, the lioness searches for a secret hideaway.

she was gentle and careful.

For the next few days, the cubs crawled about in the den, mewing like kittens, with their eyes still tightly shut. On the third day, Boto's lids opened just a crack. By the end of fifteen days, all were looking the den over in wide-eyed wonder.

Slowly, their legs grew strong enough to walk. When Boto was three weeks old, he was ready to explore the world outside the cave—and to get into trouble. One day, he saw a lizard on a rock. He pounced, trying to catch it. When the lizard ran, Boto toddled off to find it. He went too far! Lost in tall grass, he miaowed loudly. Winda found him and carried him home by the scruff of his neck.

The cubs grew playful. They wrestled, snarled, and batted each other with fat paws. They gnawed Winda's ears with sharp milk teeth and pounced on the tip of her tail when it twitched. When the cubs were not playing or sleeping, they nursed.

One day, Boto saw a huge, brown shape appear near the den. It was a lioness, but it was not his mother! Boto scrambled to Winda for protection. To his surprise, Winda seemed delighted. The two lionesses rubbed necks together, just like happy house cats. The stranger was Winda's own sister, visiting.

Lions like the company of other lions. They spend their lives in family groups, called *prides*. The pride is usually made of lionesses that are related to each other, like Winda and her sister.

There are cubs of all ages with them. One or more male lions are part of a pride, too, but the males spend much time away by themselves. A lioness with new cubs usually leaves her pride to keep the cubs hidden until they are old enough to take care of themselves among the bigger cats.

Often, Winda heard the grunting roars of her sister and other lions of her pride. She would sometimes disappear to hunt with them. She would be gone for many hours. Alone and hungry, the cubs tried to hide quietly.

Boto would wriggle into a crack between two rocks. Often, hyenas prowled nearby. Once a leopard slipped past. Such animals often kill helpless lion cubs, but luckily Winda's hiding place was not dis-

Feeding time . . .

covered. She returned at last. As soon as they heard her soft grunts, the cubs burst from hiding to welcome her.

Winda grew restless when the lions of her pride traveled to other parts of the plains. One day, when the cubs were six weeks old, she decided the time had come to bring her cubs into the pride. That morning, she gave Boto, his brother, and his sisters such a thorough licking and

and mother waits patiently while hungry nurslings drink their fill.

A lick and a promise of new adventure . . . now the young one is all ready to set out.

cleaning that their fuzzy ears burned. Then she set off, grunting to the cubs to follow.

How hard it was to follow Winda's long strides over the wild plains. They stopped only once, at a water hole, for a long and welcome drink. At last, they found the other lions of the pride. They were all together, lying in the warm sunshine. Boto sat down and stared in amazement. For a day or two, Winda kept the cubs away from the other lions. Soon, however, they became part of the family group. Now they had aunts, uncles and cousins to share their life on the plains. But the hardest part of their lives had just begun.

A flowing stream invites the thirsty family to drink, then to play and to explore.

Let's go! A pride of lions waits for the cubs to come and join them.

13

2 Lucky Boto

At seven months, Boto weighed eighty pounds and looked nearly as big as a small German shepherd dog. The baby spots had faded into the tan of a young lion. Boto still seemed like a small cub next to his two-hundred-sixty-pound mother, and even smaller next to his huge

father, who stretched nine feet from nose to tail.

Sometimes Boto tried to catch small animals and birds, bounding clumsily after them. One day, he and his sister tried to stalk a herd of wildebeests. The big antelopes turned on them, snorting and stamping. Suddenly the cubs were not so brave. They hurried back to Winda, who licked them comfortingly. They spent the afternoon in the crotch of a tree, hungry and cross.

The cubs had lived on Winda's milk until they were three months old. Lion cubs are weaned gradually after this age and begin eating meat. They tear at any scraps left by the big lions after a kill. When the pride feasted on a large animal, like a zebra, Winda

Tired cubs (above) wait for dinner.

Ah, wildebeests! (left) Get 'em!

15

often made sure her cubs got a share. If there was not enough to feed all the lions, the cubs went hungry. The adults slapped them aside. Even Winda would snarl and drive them away. Boto was learning that a lion's life is an endless struggle to get enough to eat.

Food had been scarce. The lions had roamed the plains for many days without luck, and the cubs had tasted no meat for a week. When Winda left to hunt, they went too, hoping to have a share of the meal.

In a pride, it is usually the lioness that kills the prey, although the males sometimes help to search and chase the hunted animal. Cubs stay hidden and watch. As they watch, they learn.

Boto was not yet strong or experienced enough to hunt on his own. He would not be able to do that until he was about two years old. In the meantime, he practiced. Winda was teaching him to develop his skills by letting him help stalk and bring down smaller animals. But just now, the hunting was going badly for Boto and for Winda.

The cubs were growing thin. Without food they would starve. One morning, Winda and four other

Body slung low, the lioness steals quietly across the plain, searching for food.

16

lionesses set out before dawn to stalk a herd of zebras and wildebeests. Boto and the other cubs padded behind her in the cold, dark mist. Boto could hear the zebras barking. The lionesses separated to take different paths, so the herd was soon surrounded by hunting lions, each carefully hidden in high grass.

Soon Winda dropped into the grass, belly and chin close to the ground. For more than an hour, she did not move except for the twitching of her tail. Boto felt hungry and cold, but he did not move, either.

While they lay motionless, a giraffe loped toward the herd. He paused and from his towering seventeen feet surveyed the savanna. Suddenly, without a sound of warning, he fled. The zebras stampeded. The wildebeests raced with them. Winda sprang to her feet and bounded after her prey. They were too fast . . . it was a bad night for Winda.

In the dawn light, Winda's luck changed. Near a water hole where Winda and Boto stopped to drink, a warthog, plump and juicy, kneeled on his forelegs. With the short, upturned tusks of his huge head, he dug into the ground, rooting for tubers. He

Quarry sighted, she sprints across the field. Zebras and wildebeests flee.

17

could not see Winda nor Boto. And because they were downwind, he could not smell them.

Winda inched forward. One foot. A yard. Experience told her how to judge the exact moment to charge. Suddenly, she rushed forward like a whip. The nearsighted warthog looked up and grunted in alarm.

Winda shot forward. Her fourteen-foot bound pinned the hog to the ground. When he ceased to struggle, Winda roared in triumph to the lions across the plains. The pride roared

back . . . and hurried to the feast.

Usually, such a meal was shared. But today, the older lions were bad-tempered and quarrelsome because of their great hunger. When Boto and the other cubs tried to eat, they were driven away. Half starved, they huddled together, waiting their turn.

Their turn did not come. Hyenas began to circle, drawn by their sharp sense of smell. At first, the lions charged and drove them away. The hyenas always came back. They snapped their jaws, hooted, and

The lioness has downed her prey, and a hungry male claims his share of the catch.

18

Full and happy, lioness and cub settle down on a limb to enjoy cool breezes.

made quick dashes toward the carcass. At last the adult lions had eaten enough. The hyenas seized their chance. In they rushed, snarling, fighting, snapping. Instead of defending the kill, the lions wandered off and let the hyenas claim all that now remained.

Hungry as they were, the lion cubs left to follow their mothers—all but Boto. He crouched in the shelter of some thornbushes, watching the hyenas. Others might starve, but not he. Hunger made him bold.

Boto's lips curled in a silent snarl of fury as the hyenas tore at the meat. Suddenly it was too much to watch. With a loud growl, Boto rushed among the hyenas and grabbed at a piece of meat. With a fierce yank, he ripped off a small chunk and sprinted away. Lucky Boto.

His stomach full, Boto returned to the pride. He scrambled onto the limb of an acacia tree and fell asleep. His mother joined him.

19

3 The Eyes and Ears of a Tiger

Thousands of miles from Africa's lion country, in India, a land where lions are seen only in the Gir Forest, a tigress was on the prowl. It was Tawna, a big cat, nearly eight feet long and two hundred ninety pounds. She was a handsome creature, with magnificent black stripes on a reddish tan coat.

Tawna had been hunting all night. She had followed her regular trail for miles through the dark Indian jungle, hiding in thickets. Her ears caught the faintest sounds. Her eyes spotted

A tigress ventures from her den.

the most fleeting shadows. But she had captured nothing. Now it was morning and Tawna still prowled.

As Tawna crept forward on padded paws, a monkey barked in alarm. His call warned the forest that a tiger was on the move, and there was a burst of excited activity.

Tawna emerged from her hiding place and blinked at the bright morning sun. She was tired and cross. For a week she had killed no animals to feed herself and her hungry cubs.

Tawna was hunting and traveling alone. For tigers there is no family group. The tigress provides the food for herself, and for her cubs until they are old enough to hunt for themselves. Without her they would quickly starve. Now, morning had come, but the hunt must continue.

Tawna slipped along the edge of a meadow, then down a dirt road. The hot Indian sun climbed higher in the sky. Tawna left the road and stole once again into the cool depths of the forest. This was the place she liked best, for tigers are forest cats. Here they are hidden from their prey and from the burning sun. They do not loll on the open plains the way lions do.

After a hot day's hunt, she returns.

21

Suddenly, a tiny sound made Tawna stop short. Her muscles tensed. A tiger's hearing is extremely good, and Tawna had heard the faint "whuff" of a *chital* (CHEED-ul), a kind of Indian deer. It would provide a good feast. She crouched low, chin close to thick, powerful forelegs.

Tawna's sharp vision had helped her spot the deer through the dense undergrowth. Tawna's stripes blended with the shadows and twigs of the forest. Even the patches of white above her eyes looked like dapples of sun. Her camouflage made her invisible to the deer.

Then something gave the deer a warning. A bird? A mouse darting too suddenly for cover? The deer vanished with sudden bounds, and another meal was lost.

Hot and weary, Tawna gave up hunting and began searching for her young. Their hiding place in tall grasses seemed empty because the cubs were well hidden. Even for Tawna, the cubs' black stripes and tawny coats were hard to see against the shadows of tall, sunburned grasses. The starving cubs came slowly out of hiding to greet their mother. Tawna licked them fondly.

At five months, the cubs were chunky and small, with huge paws.

Mother and cub blend against a forest of grass . . . and are hidden.

One was a female. The other two were males. Full-grown, the males would be nine feet long, or more, and weigh four hundred fifty pounds.

Until the age of three months, the cubs had lived on Tawna's milk. They were older, now, and needed meat. And they were not yet skillful enough to catch their own. Tawna must find it.

But for now, Tawna and the cubs must seek shelter from the sun. The rest of the day, they spent in the forest, curled up together, dozing.

After sunset, the forest grew cool and dark. Tawna set out once more, looking for antelope, for deer, for wild pig, for whatever might be near. To-night she must not fail! Already the cubs were weak.

Tawna's great, cushioned paws made no sound as she prowled the forest, listening and watching. Tawna's path took her to the edge of a river. For an hour, she followed its banks. At last, her sharp eyes found a buffalo herd on the river's far side. For a long time, Tawna did not move. She chose her prey, a single animal that stood apart from the others. Then she slid into the river.

Tawna swam with ease to the other side. Once on the far bank, she worked towards the buffalo, silent as a snake. At last she was close

enough. She waited, every muscle in her powerful body ready for one mighty spring. Tawna knew that if she made an error, her cubs would go hungry again.

If her aim was bad, her prey would escape. Tawna's aim was perfect. Her thick forepaw struck a blow that brought the big animal crashing to the ground, and then she killed it.

Hungry as she was, Tawna did not stop to eat. Grabbing the buffalo in strong jaws, she began dragging it backwards into thick undergrowth. She must hide it with care. This was for her starving cubs. No other animal must come near it.

When the carcass was safely hidden, Tawna started the long journey back to her waiting cubs. A sudden rain began to fall and the water came down in torrents. Tawna padded through the wet foliage, seeking her cubs. With loud, rasping grunts she called them again and again. They must start back now, at once, to claim the food.

Where were they? Where were the cubs hiding? Tawna roared . . . and they came to her, slowly, through the pounding rain.

Tawna turned and began pushing

Swimming's good—to cool off or to travel to new hunting areas.

through the high growth. The cubs knew they were to follow. By the time they reached the river, it was swollen and angry. The swiftly flowing water pushed the young tigers downstream, but they fought their way valiantly across to the other bank.

With strength born of excitement and the hope of food, the cubs scrambled· behind Tawna. The tigress led them into the thicket and . . . there it was. The carcass lay untouched, waiting for the cubs . . . who would survive, for another week.

With one swipe of her steely claw (left), the tigress snares a young water buffalo.

Mother's half-grown cubs (next page) eagerly share the kill.

Saving Lions and Tigers

If you visit Africa and happen to meet a lion wearing a collar, don't be startled. There is a tiny radio in that collar that bleeps.

By picking up the signals, scientists, like George Schaller (right) and his assistant, are able to follow a lion to learn about his way of life: where he hunts and sleeps, and what he eats. With this and other vital information, land can be set aside that will provide a healthy life for these remarkable cats.

But what about the tiger? He is in danger, now, as man clears away jungles in Asia. He, too, is being studied—to find ways to save him.

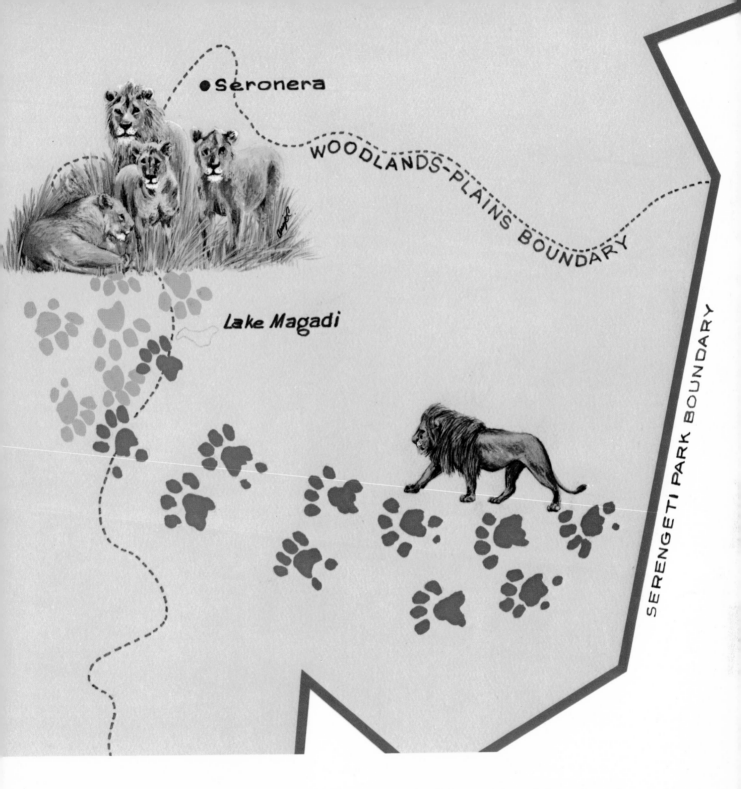

Seronera

WOODLANDS-PLAINS BOUNDARY

Lake Magadi

SERENGETI PARK BOUNDARY

Most lions live in prides. A few are wanderers, nomads. Using radio bleeps as their guide, scientists followed some of the nomads (blue paw prints, above). Eventually, one of the wanderers joined a pride (upper left portion of map).

29

WHERE LIONS

AFRICA

Equator

LIONS ●

The **LION**, once king of Asia Minor, Europe, and Africa, today rules only over **CENTRAL** and **SOUTHERN AFRICA** and the tiny **GIR FOREST OF INDIA**.

AND TIGERS LIVE

TIGERS

TIGERS, fast disappearing, prowl the jungles of **INDIA** and **SOUTH-EAST ASIA** and the colder forests of **KOREA, MANCHURIA** and **SIBERIA**. Small numbers are found elsewhere in **Asia**.

31

WHEN YOU SEE A LION OR A TIGER

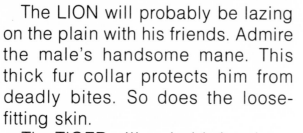

The LION will probably be lazing on the plain with his friends. Admire the male's handsome mane. This thick fur collar protects him from deadly bites. So does the loose-fitting skin.

The TIGER will probably be alone, staring back from behind tall reeds. Admire his stripes . . . black on a reddish or yellow background. They come to a point along his spine, but his sides have a random pattern, ideal for jungle hiding. Markings of two tigers are always similar, but never exactly the same.

Note the long whiskers on both cats. These feelers help the cats prowl silently through underbrush.

But beware of the incisors—sharp teeth for digging into flesh and for tearing. And beware of the paws, softly padded for silent stalking, but armed with razor-sharp claws that spring into action.

Don't be misled by the great cats' yawns. The lion is sometimes lazy, the tiger is sometimes shy—but not when they are hungry.